PIANO / VOCAL / GUITAR

# THE LORAX: MUSIC FROM THE MOTION PICTURE SOUNDTRACK

## Dr. Seuss'
## The LORAX

### Original Songs by John Powell and Cinco Paul
### Score Composed by John Powell

ISBN 978-1-4584-8804-6

### HAL•LEONARD®
### CORPORATION

7777 W. BLUEMOUND RD. P.O. BOX 13819 MILWAUKEE, WI 53213

Visit Hal Leonard Online at
**www.halleonard.com**

# LET IT GROW
## (Celebrate The World)

Music and Lyrics by ESTER DEAN,
CHRISTOPHER "TRICKY" STEWART,
JOHN POWELL, CINCO PAUL
and AARON PEARCE

**Moderate Dance groove**

Plant a seed ___ in -
Just be - lieve ___ and you're

side the earth. ___ Just one way ___ to know it's worth ___ when we
al - most there. ___ Use your heart ___ to show you care. ___ Come on and

# THNEEDVILLE

Music by JOHN POWELL
Lyrics by CINCO PAUL

# THIS IS THE PLACE
## (Tricky Version)

Music by JOHN POWELL
Lyrics by CINCO PAUL

# EVERYBODY NEEDS A THNEED

Music by JOHN POWELL
Lyrics by CINCO PAUL

**ONCE-LER:** Ev - 'ry - bod - y needs a Thneed, _____ a fine thing that all _____ peo - ple... _____

**TEEN BOY 1:** *You know what we need? For you to stop!*

**TEEN BOY 2:** *Yeah, you suck!*

**TEEN BOY 3:** *Yeah!*

CROWD:

Ah, ah, ah, ah.

Ev-'ry-bod-y needs a Thneed! __

A fine thing that all _____ peo - ple need!

The Thneed is good! The Thneed is great! Let's hope we're

# HOW BAD CAN I BE

Music by JOHN POWELL
Lyrics by CINCO PAUL
and ALLAN PETER GRIGG

ba-a-a-ad can I be? I'm just fol-low-ing my des-ti-ny. How

ba-a-a-ad can I be? I'm just do-ing what comes_ nat-'ral-ly. How

ba-a-a-ad can I be? How bad can I pos-sib-ly be? Well there's a

prin-ci-ple in na-ture **ONCE-LER:** that al-most ev-'ry crea-ture knows, _ called "sur-
**FAMILY:** (Prin-ci-ple in na-ture.)

# LET IT GROW

Music by JOHN POWELL
Lyrics by CINCO PAUL

**Slowly, freely**

Em    A    D

**O'HARE:**

time to let it grow. My name's O' - Hare, I'm one of

Dsus    D    A/C#    Bm    A

you. I live here _____ in Th - need - ville too. _____ The

G    D/F#    Bm

things you say _____ just might be true. _____ It could be time _____ to

A/C#    G    Csus2/E

start a - new _____ and may - be change _____ my point _____ of view. _____

**Moderate Country 2 feel**

**Freely. slowly**

**Moderate Gospel feel**

44

reap what you don't sow. _____ It's just one ti - ny seed __

but it's all we real - ly need. __ It's time to ban - ish all your greed. I -

mag - ine Thneed-ville flow'red and treed. Let this be our sol - emn

**Slowly, with feeling**

creed. We say let it

# LET IT GROW
## (Original Demo)

Music by JOHN POWELL
Lyrics by CINCO PAUL

# FUNERAL FOR A TREE

Music by JOHN POWELL

**Slowly, expressively**

*\* Recorded a half step higher.*

**Moderately slow**